Unknown England

Unknown England

Introduction & commentaries by
Ian Niall

Photographs by
Kenneth Scowen

B T Batsford Ltd London

Frontispiece *Winter landscape near Houghton, Sussex*

Filmset by Asco Trade Typesetting Ltd, Hong Kong
Printed by South China Printing Co. Hong Kong
for the publishers B.T. Batsford Ltd
4 Fitzhardinge Street, London WIH OAH

ISBN 0 7134 1843 5

Contents

Introduction
Kenneth Scowen's England

Photography is not simply a dimension of art. In its many forms it
can be appreciated panoramically and in stereo, but its subtlety as a
form of art lies in the ability of the photographer to stimulate the
thought, to make the viewer see what he sees, and to imagine, on
most occasions, that without the stimulus he would himself have
seen and appreciated the subject. For a long time now Kenneth
Scowen's art has delighted me when I have discovered it on the front
of *Country Life* or on my own weekly page in the magazine for which
I have written for more than a quarter of a century. Often I have
recognized a Scowen without looking at his name at the right-hand
bottom corner of his picture. He is the kind of photographer who
puts his distinctive mark on his work and a man whose admirers
know his mark. Just as a painter takes the viewer into his landscape
and leads him onwards, fascinated and stimulated by what has been
suggested, a talented cameraman takes hold of his 'audience' and
Scowen has taken hold of those who look for his published work.
His photography has the same quality no matter what his subject
may be, a tree in the Vale of Evesham at blossom time, the spire of
Salisbury, rotund oasthouses in Kent, or the magnificent contours of
a windmill in East Anglia. It is often the habit of a particular class of
photographer to fire off shot after shot, and use rolls of film loaded in
two or even three cameras hung about their necks, trusting that some
fleeting expression on the face of their subject may be fortuitously
captured to complement a contrived pose. Snap-shotting is perhaps
the last resort of the man who acknowledges his lack of patience and
his inability to control his material, and indeed most photographers
accept that this is so. Scowen's work and the work of other brilliant
photographers of the same school gives one the impression that he
always knew, and always knows what he wants. He finds his view-
point and knows the angle, waits for the light and the shadow
and the thing is on film, but it is never even as simple as that. Most
of what is art in photography depends on the 'third eye' in the way
that a picture depends on what is in the eye of the painter, the use of
chords depends on the music in the head of the composer, the words
that continually arrange and rearrange themselves in the mind of a
poet. Scowen is a professional of course, and not a dilettante
photographer dallying with a camera. He labours under the necessity
of pleasing his publishers and a high standard of professionalism sets
him apart. He knows what pleases. He even convinces his publishers
that this is what they were seeking. In the careful selection of his
work included here some pictures that would have pleased the public

undoubtedly didn't please the man who made them. He was, after all, sifting through his best work to give us *Unknown England*. His publisher almost certainly had a few tactful suggestions to make about marrying one picture with another. The outcome is something out of the run of ordinary picture books.

When I was sent the proofs of the pictorial work included in this book, so that I might add a word or two by way of introduction, I recognized the futility of attempting to say something about technical competence. Long ago it dawned on me that I was a lost photographer when a great exponent of both the wide-angle plate camera, and the miniature, revealed to me the single-mindedness it takes to make a photographic artist. If I said anything about Scowen's photography it would contribute little and represent only my unresearched conclusion. There are a great many first-class pictures in this collection. It is difficult to put a general label on them. They are pictorial and architectural to a certain degree. Scowen's composition is born of his artistic sense and his ability to illustrate—and there I must stop. The photographs offered have been grouped under different headings, eleven in all. It is obvious that the when and where that produced many of them sprang from Mr Scowen's professional needs or from commissions. One day he took

Near Sudbury, Suffolk

8

Near Winchester, Hampshire

a wonderful picture of All Souls, Oxford. An entirely different
inspiration produced a Sussex landscape and the old world village
street in Hampshire. There is nothing to say when. It may have been
a day later or a month before another of his masterpieces of
illustration.

The device of grouping these photographs under different headings
will not prevent the person who takes up the book flipping from
one section to another. It is inevitable that this should happen in
handling any picture book. Scowen's publisher has elected to call the
production *Unknown England*. Everyone, it might be said, knows the
Shambles in York, Salisbury Cathedral, Symonds Yat or Anne
Hathaway's Cottage, but of course everyone doesn't, although each
one of us may know England in part. It is impossible to give a

Winter sunset, Surrey

picture of the whole or to give a series of pictures that might pass as
the whole, and being particularly aware of this, I think perhaps we
are talking about Kenneth Scowen's England in which he has given
us the idyllic scene at Cuddestone Mill on the Thames, a yellow-
lighted Regency lamp standard to vie with the sun being quenched
in the sea beyond the promenade at Brighton, coves of Cornwall,
Trinity Great Court at Cambridge, and the Tudor beauty of the old
master weaver's house at Dedham in Essex. Somewhere in the pages
turned we will all come upon the familiar scene for Kenneth Scowen
has been there to watch the thatcher on the roof, the hurdle-maker at
his trade. He has admired the poplars lining the wheatfield in Suffolk,
and found one kind of beauty on the Military Canal at Appledore
and another on the river at Clifton Hampden.

Downland slopes, Sussex

Symond's Yat, Herefordshire

The Dimensions
of Landscape

To talk of English landscape is to indulge in a somewhat fanciful
exercise because, like the English village, it is something that cannot
be exactly defined. It is a many-splendoured thing, to use the lyric
writer's words, one of such variety that everyone has a different,
cherished image of a particular corner of a county or even a parish.
The dilemma of the man who would illustrate England is not just
where to begin, but where to end. Even so, if the thing is done
comprehensively there must remain, unselected, as many ideal, idyllic
views, as many framings of the landscape, as those picked out. There
is really no typical English scene, yet a great many people have their
conception of it framed in their minds. It may be a recollection of a
view of the Malvern Hills, Salisbury Plain, a smoky, deep purple
twilight or a Turner painting with a romantic, delicate haze. Every
visitor carries away his own England, gathered, like hedgerow
flowers, while he or she drove down through the Moonraker country
and the green hills of Somerset, crossed the wonderful slab bridges
the men of Devon built to ford the turbulent streams of their
moorland, or trundled cautiously down Porlock Hill. The big sky of
East Anglia, the flat country of the Fens, is a black-earth, market
garden, criss-crossed with slow-flowing drains, treed here and there
by snake-skinned silver birches, and that is England for people who
love this kind of horizon. The man who wants a warmer scene, a
different aspect of civilized influence, looks for it in the softer
landscape of the Home Counties and doesn't go hurrying north to
the Pennines where he might conjure up a violent period in history
when the Romans left Hadrian's Wall. The poet who wrote for a
homesick Englishman said that whoever awakens in England in
April finds the elm tree bole in tiny leaf. Housman saw the western
landscape and the hills of the Welsh Border, but a sentimentalist
might find even more to dream on in a collection of photographic
viewpoints, which some people may recognize and others wonder
about. There is more, much more, to England than the magic lantern
world seen from a speeding inter-city train. When all is said and
done, a thousand times more than may be seen on a hostelling
holiday, the long-distance walk round the Lizard, the Ridgeway, or
the track that takes a walker from Edale in Derbyshire north to
Yetholm where the Pennine way ends. Nor is it all in the viewfinder
of everyone's camera. Even the skilled photographer captures a thing
that is immediate, the shadows of clouds crossing hills, like a frown
of perplexity on a human face, expanding sunlight bathing a valley in
brightness like a happy smile, or the clear, cold austerity of winter, a

Summer landscape, Southrepps, Norfolk

filigree of leafless trees against a hard sky. Pictures that stimulate such thought are inspirational in the proper meaning of the word, and in landscape what is photographed may be time set. Perhaps once in a thousand days the scene with its particular light, its cloud, its shadows, may be momentarily exactly the same, but it could as well be an unrepeatable thing, like a taste of honey with a unique, never again flavour.

Some people have a penchant for a landscape entirely in contrast to that of their native district, even when they live in attractive surroundings, so that a man of Kent may have a liking for the fells of Cumbria, or one from Somerset may be fascinated by the flat country of the Wash. The southern counties, the Downs, the green belt area, and places designated, not as national parks, but areas of outstanding beauty, have a certain order, a particular kind of patchwork of park and woodland characteristic of a more settled, residential part of the country. Here generations of merchants, businessmen, and a great many retired military men and civil servants, live within easy reach of London. Their residences, large and not so large, dot the area. It is only an hour from sweet Sussex by the sea to the centre of London or from the Surrey hills along the valley of the Thames. Stockbrokers and city tycoons commute from places in the country every day, dictating letters on the way, and sometimes talking on the telephone as their chauffeurs steer them up the Brighton Road or the M4. It is hard to appreciate that part of London's working population comes from out-lying places like Guildford, or Lewes, losing itself for a time in the great ant hill but emerging again, at the end of the day, to go back into a peaceful world beyond suburbia. At weekends too, the Londoner himself trundles out to admire the landscape, country churches, the oasthouses of Kent, the autumn scene where ponies browse, or a footpath through the standing wheat. Once this green hinterland could only be reached when the Londoner took his annual holiday. Many of the scenic gems of the southern counties remained for a long time undiscovered by the majority of people who travelled by train. Still farther back it was the stage coach or shanks pony that took the city dweller out in search of his heritage. Now the whole population of the city moves out thanks to the motorcar, farther and farther into the depths of the country.

The choice of vistas is an unlimited one. Farther out, beyond the

The lighthouse at Happisburgh, Norfolk

In the Surrey hills looking towards Ranmore

Looking to Headley church, Surrey

home counties, are thousands more, and, even today, secluded, secret
places where time seems to stand still and the bell tolls as it did in
medieval times. Here, while a wisp of smoke drifts from a cottage
chimney, silence can be almost oppressive and the visitor imagine
himself an intruder, a trespasser in a private world. The variety of
landscape suggests that people live in a different way and derive their
character from their particular surroundings, as they do in Suffolk
and Norfolk. The very atmosphere has a timelessness about it, as
though nothing has ever changed, and nothing ever will, but a train
once rumbled to a halt and jetted steam across the now weed-grown
platform at a place called Potter Heigham. The porter, who might
also have been the station-master, shouted the train's destination and
young country lads shouldered their kitbags and left for the war,
while the very air vibrated with the passing of bombers on their way
to Germany. But if this eastern countryside has little appeal, one may

Autumn near Mickleham, Surrey

leave and journey west and south, through Oxfordshire and the Cotswolds, Chipping Camden in Gloucestershire, on the way to Herefordshire, the apple orchards, Symonds Yat and the Monnow Valley, or down south into Hampshire, to Winchester, the one time capital city, and then north again to an even older part—Mercia in which lay Avebury of the standing stones, Silbury and the Sanctuary, places at which history was written in blood, never on paper. The West Country draws people in hundreds of thousands to sample scrumpy and clotted cream, and to admire picturesque cottages and villages of Devon, where Dan'el Witton, Peter Gurney and Harry 'awk, along with one or two others, went to Widecombe Fair, all out-along, down-along lea. Northwards, a different place and a different topography, Lathkildale in the Peak District, between Matlock and Bakewell, or in more rugged country still, near Crook in Westmorland or Rydal Fell seen from Ambleside.

Apple blossom and oasthouses near Tonbridge, Kent

21

On Headley Heath, Surrey

In the Monnow Valley, Herefordshire

The Lake District: Rydal Fell near Ambleside

Disused railway station at Potter Heigham, Norfolk

From a bridge over the Lathkil in Lathkildale, Derbyshire

Above left *Cotswold landscape near Chipping Campden, Gloucestershire*

Left *Dartmoor: Widecombe from Bonehill Down, Devonshire*

Prehistoric stone circle at Avebury, Wiltshire

Near Crook, Westmorland

Ancient Fabrics

What may be called ancient fabrics, often the period architecture of England as it was when history was first recorded, attracts a great many people concerned for and interested in the things of the past. The old buildings, grand mansions and castles also occupy the attention of the enthusiastic and sometimes inspired photographer. What a castle is is not so easily defined as some people might imagine. Some castles were specially designed forts to withstand siege. Some, called castles, were fortified manors and in this realm the fortification of an abbey tower might be construed to be a kind of castle, and towers along the northern border are also sometimes thought to be castles. The purist would say that the Romans built forts. The Saxons barely qualified as castle-builders. It was the Normans who built the real castles of England, and theirs is the strongest influence, surviving that of Romans and Saxons who held parts of Britain in their day. The castle continued to be built and to be modified for centuries after England absorbed the Normans. The Norman ground plan of moat and bailey, the mound, inner and outer defences, made their castles formidable obstacles to military conquest. Even after the siege gun rendered the Norman plan obsolete, some Norman castles are entirely recognizable for what they were when William and his heirs built them. The Conqueror lost no time in marching on worthwhile forts the Saxons had occupied and defended and thereafter the Normans built both castles and churches in a manner that testified to military genius and devotion to God.

Carisbrooke on the Isle of Wight was one of the places that commended itself to the Normans for there they built a priory and a church which housed the Benedictines. They also built a castle, inspired in this case perhaps, by the fact that the Romans in their day had fortified the site. Carisbrooke Castle was built into English history. In Tudor times when the king of Spain thought to emulate the Normans and take England by sending his Armada to do battle against the English fleet, Carisbrooke was refurbished as a stronghold. But it was later on that it became celebrated, not as a castle that had withstood a siege, but as a prison. Here Charles I was incarcerated for two years before his execution. Here too, his wretched offspring, Prince Henry and Princess Elizabeth were held prisoners, and here they died.

Carisbrooke Castle, Isle of Wight

Not every castle gets into the history book as the scene of dramatic event, however. Some, it must be said, are monuments to pretentiousness on the part of the man who built them. Eastnor Castle would not deceive the connoisseur of architecture or the student of history, and yet it looks like a kind of castle. This is because it is a castellated mansion in Norman and Gothic style. It was built, however, no farther back than the nineteenth century and it houses armour and tapestries which perhaps give it a certain credibility. Guildford's Castle survives as a ruin of medieval origin, but one of no great historical significance, for all its antiquity, but not so far away, as the messenger might have ridden, William the Conqueror built a castle that was to become almost certainly the most celebrated castle in the world. What William built was soon obscured, overlaid by what the planners of today would call subsequent development. Windsor became popular in Tudor times. Henry III's concern was to fortify and improve defences. Edward III thought to improve the royal apartments and to build a Chapel for the Order of the Garter. The dynasties which followed did more to change the face of this splendid castle. Charles II, George II, George IV and Queen Victoria in her day, all embellished and improved the royal residence, the outward appearance of which changed greatly in nineteenth-century renovations that increased the height of the round tower. Who has not heard of Windsor hasn't heard of the kings and queens of England over a period of five hundred years or more.

In the appropriateness of phrases a palace is fit for a queen, but not every palace was built for a queen, or for a bishop of the church. Sir John Vanbrugh designed his palace on behalf of the nation so that England might fittingly reward Marlborough. The Duke's even more illustrious descendant, Sir Winston Churchill, was born there in 1874. In one of the great palace's lesser bedrooms personal relics of Winston Churchill are preserved. In larger state apartments there are others of different sorts, tapestries, fine china, portraits and furniture in keeping with such works of art. Queen Anne's gardener had a

Windsor Castle, Berkshire: the East Front

33

Guildford Castle, Surrey

hand in planning the layout of the grounds and thought to emulate
the French style to be seen at Versailles and Vaux-le-Vicomte, but
before the monstrosity of formality was properly done Capability
Brown was asked to apply his own idea to the setting. He transform-
ed the whole thing with his talent for landscaping, using trees and
lawn, and contriving to make the place look natural. He went further
and harnessed the River Glynne to give Blenheim its lake and Henry
Wise's influence was totally inverted.

Not every historic building survives to satisfy generations of
architects the way Bodiam in Sussex has done. Bodiam Castle is

Bodiam Castle, Sussex

certainly something of an inspiration for the man with a camera, and goes back to the fourteenth century when Richard II licensed its building. The French had raided and pillaged both Rye and Winchelsea and some military support seemed to be necessary. Bodiam, however, never needed to man its battlements, or dip its well to check the water, for it was never attacked, which accounts for its fine state of preservation. It may well have been that the nobleman who was given licence to build it thought more about the impregnability of his castle than its strategic situation isolated in the country—in the middle of an artificially created lake.

Blenheim Palace, Oxfordshire

Eastnor Castle, Herefordshire

By the Waterside

As an island race it is natural for the English to love to be beside the seaside. When they can't make an excursion to the coast by train, by coach or private car, and don't happen to live beside the sea, they love to dally by the river, to go to the lake, the Serpentine, the canal. To be by the waterside is relaxing and it doesn't really matter where it is so long as the surroundings are reasonably congenial. Even when the canals, to which more people turn now in search of recreational outlets, were important lines of commerce not all of them, along their complete lengths, were throughfares through grime and muck. There was always colour, the greenery of rushes or thorn hedges, carpets of weed, in some places, and yellow flags to mark the way. People who were within walking distance were drawn to the canals to watch the boat people passing, towed by the towpath nag, leaving a churned wake when the boat had an engine to carry it, by means of simple hydraulics and the operation of lock gates, to a higher or lower level. Not many people who respond to such things bother to search for their reasons. The seaside, 'beside the sea', was a popular Edwardian concert party chorus and that particular dream was epitomised in a trip for the Cockney family, down Canvey or Southend, as they would say, or a basinful of the briny at Brighton. It had been there long before the Brighton line was laid down, of course. Brighton came alive in the days of the Prince Regent and the extravagance of his day which gave the resort a unique character, something as much to do with history as the Tudor image Henry VIII gave Hampton Court. A time was when all the world was at Brighton, strolling along the prom, looking down at the waves from the pier, admiring itself in the pavilion, fashionable young ladies and their protectors, families of more than averagely affluent citizens who stayed in the boarding houses and trekked to and fro to test the temperature of the water from the steps of a bathing machine. All the world included sellers of whelks, touts and pickpockets and the purveyors of naughty postcards. All this is suggested, it may fairly be claimed, by a distant prospect of the sea and the pier and the setting sun, with a lamp, already lit to enliven the night, and adorned as lamps were in both Edwardian and Victorian times, with decorative cast-iron.

If the noise and hullabaloo of the overcrowded belle of the southern

Brighton, Sussex: the Palace Pier at sunset

The river Adur, Sussex

resorts is too much for the nerves of some people there remains more
than enough coastline, west and northwards to satisfy the most
discriminating of holidaymakers without the money to fly to the
far Pacific islands or down to the Costa del Sol. Some choose to go
in hopeful search for the undiscovered coves of Cornwall as painted
(in the off-season) by artists who crowd one another to produce their
oils and watercolours of sea, sand and sky, and old cottages looking
at boats that nudge each other at the rise and fall of the tide, serving,
between times, perhaps, as perches for solitary gulls. The whole of
the West Country is a magnet to draw the tourist to the beaches, to
beautiful rivers that drain the high country moors of Exe and Dart
and carry in flood from over-brimming pools and weirs, fronds of
fern, leaves of trees and feathers of waterfowl that hang where the
freshwater and the sea meet at the estuary moorings. In another place
is another scene, like Durdle Door in Dorset, that impressive mass of

Chichester, Sussex: the harbour

rock-carving produced by the sea and the gales, or Chichester
Harbour. Here, long ago, the Roman soldiers stood sentry and, in
the course of time, Normans too, came to make their military
presence felt and build a cathedral.

Inland the pattern of communications derives from the draining of
uplands by streams and rivers alongside which roads grew from
tracks and bridleways. The long valley of the Thames has buried the
bones of the warriors and the kings of Mercia, and before them, the
tribes that ruled Britain even before words were written to record
history. The Thames wound its peaceful way out of the very heart of
England to divide the land kings would fight over, the counties of
Oxford and Berkshire, Middlesex and Surrey. During the Industrial
Revolution our forefathers built a canal to come by stages down to
the very mouth of the Thames, but industry that was spawned in the
Midlands didn't penetrate too far up the great river, with all its locks

The river Exe, Devon

and weirs. Civilised England has its proper place on the upper reaches, beyond Marlow and Henley, and Spenser's *Sweet Thames* flows nowhere more sweetly than here. What could be more enchanting than the arches of a river bridge in the green of the Oxfordshire landscape, or the pastoral peace in which a man sits fishing at a place called Cuddesdon Mill?

Not everyone is moved by the peace and serenity of a southern landscape, however. There are people who look for beauty of a different kind, beauty that inspired lakeland poets who wrote of a wilder scene, the Cumbrian landscape, and more rugged wilderness than anything suggested by Cotswold or Chiltern Hills. Here live a different race of Englishmen, imprinted by a different environment, and more at home in the grandeur of crags and steep fells than in the valley of a slow, meandering river with a hundred bridges. Lakeland

The river Thame at Cuddesdon Mill, Oxfordshire

Porthcurno, Cornwall

is named for its waters and meres—Derwentwater, Windermere,
Ullswater, Elterwater, Thirlmere, Wastwater and Grasmere. At every
turn of the snaking, valley roads is a new vista of scrub oaks, reeds
and rushes fringing another lake or mere. Here Wordsworth tailored
his verses and recited them aloud, carried away by the daffodils and
the breeze, stopped in his tracks by the face of a mountain hazed in a
mist of rain that makes this the greenest countryside in the whole of
England. Yet they come here in their thousands, the fell-walkers, the
campers, the tourists who would walk where poets walked, taste
Grasmere gingerbread and Kendal mint. This too, is England,
though it may be a far cry from bank holiday on the beach at
Brighton, the canal at Stockton Bridge or that flat landscape across
which the Royal Military Canal sluggishly moves at Appledore in
Kent.

Durdle Door, near Lulworth, Dorset

The Thames at Clifton Hampden, Oxfordshire

The Dart Estuary at Dartmouth, Devonshire

Cadgwith, Cornwall

The Royal Military Canal at Appledore, Kent

The Grand Union Canal at Stockton Bridge, Warwickshire

Elterwater, Westmorland

The Nature of Villages

Planning, for most of us, is a word with almost sinister overtones because its outcome either restricts our freedom or over-rides our hopes of preserving what we have. In the case of the villages in which a few fortunate people are able to live there is nowadays none of the unplanned development that made them in the first place, but planning control doesn't necessarily operate to give us old-world atmosphere or to maintain it. Industry, near at hand, may ensure the survival of the community but it always destroys the close-knitness of the human fabric. Villages that remain unspoilt tend to acquire a scarcity value and their enchantment is thereby enhanced. Such gems on the patchwork of the country can never be created, either at the stroke of the planner's pen, or by the will of parliament. Both influences may create new towns and try their hands at garden cities, but the truth is that the English village is a spore growth. It grew, long ago, where conditions were particularly suitable, around the mill, the church, the drovers' inn, a quarry or a lookout place where in ancient times there was a tribal boundary or frontier. There is really no typical English village because each one is an original. From these minor settlements the towns and cities were stocked, and there is little more to be said about them that doesn't depend on a kind of Dreamthorpe. We all have our own image of the perfect village, an idyllic one. It is a cluster of old cottages and a village green with a duckpond. It is a church, a few trees with a rookery; a winding street with gables and chimneypots of different designs, or a place with a painted inn sign above a low doorway and a door with centuries of black paint on it covered by a film of dust. We know it because we carry it in the mind. It goes with the scent of wood-smoke. It is Tudor with timbers, wattle and daub, thatch or heavy slate nailed on a ridge as uneven as the backbone of a prehistoric monster. We find it, and it becomes real because we drink the potion and follow Alice through the tiny door. What we are most fascinated by is the 'belonging' of villagers in their village where everyone is like a relative and no one has a private life. The man who comes out from the high-rise city does so because he belongs nowhere in the canyons. He finds that beer tastes different when he drinks it from a battered pewter tankard in the village pub. He almost belongs when the villager gives him a cordial good-day. If he sits long enough among the locals, who knows, he might just begin to be one of them, and at closing time stand talking in the village street, looking up at the stars and hearing the clock chime in the nearest cottage. Villages have to be romantic places. It is in their nature to be so to the outsider and

Worcestershire half-timberwork

The New Inn, Pembridge, Herefordshire

the visitor. The connoisseur of villages has his own district, a part of the world where the little places fill the bill, and have that special something about them that appeals not just to a sense of the romantic but to an artist's eye. So it is that there are people who love Devon villages like North Bovey, white and clean, the warm stone of Stanton in Gloucestershire, the thatch of Luccombe in Somerset, or Milton Abbas in Dorset, the medieval character of a little place near Pershore, or the New Inn and the not-so-new Tudor timbers, blackly framing a white façade.

It can never be said that when you have seen one English village you have seen them all. The enchantment, the charm of them is endless, and, saving the intervention of the planners and the drivers of motorways with their bulldozers, everlasting. England is its villages

Regency model village: Milton Abbas, Dorset

for a great many people whose native places have been rebuilt and renovated out of recognition so that they might stay abreast of the times. If they were concerned to stay abreast of the times in Cavendish in Suffolk they didn't alter the acute pitch of the roof of thatched cottages about the church, and in Smarden in Kent they kept the oasthouse. At Westwell in Oxfordshire, and in many other little places in the same part of the world, they kept the pond. A village should have a pond and a green on which the cricket team can play. At Hambledon they carefully preserved the rules of cricket, for Hambledon Cricket Club is in the history book as the forerunner of the MCC itself. Here they laid down the law long ago about the popping of the crease, and the dimensions of a wicket, though the American visitor may wonder what it was all about, and if it really

Tredington, Warwickshire

mattered. A stream flows through Abinger in Surrey. In summer
laburnum festoons the branches of trees that overhang the street in
Weobley in Herefordshire. You make your journey. You take
your pick, for there is blossom in the streets of Tredington in
Warwickshire, Amberley in Sussex, or Stoke Gabriel in Devon. And,
if the village is an altogether different conception, perhaps as you
cruise through it you stop to admire such a place as Burwash in
Sussex, or Zennor, in Cornwall of the Cromlechs, a village that looks
to the sea on the road westward from St Ives. It is the nature of the
English village to be beautiful, to be full of nostalgia, to have
perhaps, the remains of a village pump, an old smithy, a village hall
and, in the past, a village idiot to give baffling answers to the
townsman with a particularly cunning obtuseness. Down there, the

Cotswold stone at Stanton, Gloucestershire

Burwash, Sussex

townsman knows, time stands still. The swifts skim eternally round the church tower, dogs sleep on flags and nothing ever happens. Some things, of course, are not recorded on the photographic emulsion. Some things are pictures in the mind, fixed with a solution that makes them that they never fade.

Abinger, Surrey

Cavendish, Suffolk

Hambledon, Hampshire

Amberley, Sussex

Luccombe, Somerset

63

Zennor, Cornwall

Smarden, Kent

Weobley, Herefordshire

Stoke Gabriel and the river Dart, Devonshire

The village pond, Westwell, Oxfordshire

North Bovey, Devonshire

The Old, Unsatanic Mills

Even the present-day generation of country dwellers tends to be only half aware of the part that mills, which long ago dotted the length and breadth of England, once played in both the domestic and national economy of their country. Mills were nearly all within a day's travel in the day of the ox and the working horse. A cart or a wagon of corn, from the most recent threshing or brought from the security of the high granary, would be led to the mill. A day's travel would see the cartload there with grain, which would often be immediately exchanged for already milled wheat or oats. This was a special kind of reciprocal business between miller and farmer involving most of the other local farmers in the handing-on of the product of their labour. The corn mills of old depended for their power on the great sails with which they were equipped, or on a waterwheel in a mill-race leading from a stream or a millpond. The sails of the mill, or its waterwheel, were geared to the millstone, sometimes by a series of belts transmitting power to shafting and sometimes by a crownwheel and shaft. Nearly all the working mills had gone by the middle of the present century. The jolly miller himself had become a legend. The milling of flour had become big business in an age when the village baker, too, let his fire go out but time was when the miller himself was one of the most important men in his community. He was never done milling, autumn, winter, spring or summer, for corn was first brought to him after threshing, and then, as the farm needed feedstuff or the market was ready for flour at a proper price. A fair amount of grain was always kept in farm granaries as a kind of hedge against inflation or against a famine before another harvest. The windmill turned inexpensively and sometimes a turret actually enabled it to be set to catch the wind. It tended to be a landmark with upstretched arms and its sails turned merrily in a high wind, slowly and peacefully in the more gentle currents of air. Its height, or the situation of the structure, put its sails in a wind that moved the topmost branches of lofty trees and whistled round the steeple of the church, making the weathercock spin. A corn mill, whatever its kind, is always particularly impressive when it is working, for then it has a life of its own. The miller pulls a lever, engages the train of wheels, cogs and belt-driven shafting, and the mill immediately has a heartbeat and a belly rumble. There is a vibration in the very structure which a man feels from the soles of his feet to the top of his head. The mill takes command. It is no longer under the hand of the miller. He becomes its servant, hauling up fat-bellied sacks from the very bowels of the thing, to pour their

Outwood Mill, Surrey: the oldest working mill in England

contents into a chute that spills the grain in a steady trickle in the way of the millstone. Down on another floor the hurrying miller bags up the flour in more closely-woven sacks and hurries up to feed the hungry maw of the thing again. It is a no less exciting business for the man who stands in the watermill, for the rush of water is music that accompanies his labour, fills in the background of groaning journals and rumbling cogwheels, dusted with flour drifting in the air like pollen from the trees. The enormous water-wheel rumbles and rattles on, spilling weed and dribbling the 'light ale' of the stream like the oldest inhabitant drinking up his pint at closing time. The building of the mill moves with what seem to be never-ending earth tremors caused by the operation of the enormous machine.

There are advocates of conservation at every step along the modern road, and none more deserving of praise than those who turn a nostalgic eye on the old corn mills which time and circumstance have fortuitously left us. We should preserve them for more than senti-mental reasons, for they have a simple lesson for us. They are powered by the natural elements in the water of the millrace or the wind that has blown across the surface of this earth since time began, and the conservationists who talk about the energy crisis, pollution and the drying up of oil wells, might think back to what was so economically achieved in days long gone. Collectors of mills go out

At Cley-next-the-Sea, Norfolk

in search of them as some people go in search of historic churches, castles and the sites of ancient battles. They have all kinds to choose from. There are marsh mills in East Anglia. The tallest mill in England stands, nine storeys high, in Norfolk. There is a fine tide mill in Suffolk, a brick tower mill at Stanstead, and a very fine round tower of a mill at Cley-next-the-sea, also in Norfolk where windmills abound. At Fladbury Mill, in Worcestershire, the river turns a waterwheel. The name rings a bell, for at another watermill Constable stayed to paint The Hay Wain—Flatford Mill in Suffolk. In other places there are different mills, and the relics of many old mills that no longer turn, waterwheels that have grown green slime on their wooden parts, their ironwork fused together by rust. Some of the better preserved mills still have spars and sails. The mill at Outwood in Surrey is a fine sight, and the fact it is there is one of the minor wonders of a century in which the steam engine and even the internal combustion engine, have tended to become obsolete. We love the extravagance of our throw-away age and who but a Quixotic character would think to have windmills grinding corn for England in the twenty-first century? Yet it may come to that.

Fladbury Mill, Worcestershire

The Rural Scene

What happens in the rural scene is as fascinating as the landscape itself for anyone who goes in search of the essentials of life in the country, for here people enjoy the unhurried tenor of their way. Here they have their being and earn their living doing largely pastoral things like harvesting, practising the crafts their fathers taught them, being entertained by the things their fathers loved. Where else can people watch a travelling Morris of dancers perform as well as they do in a country setting? Where else is cricket ever played in so relaxed and happy a fashion as on the village green where things have always been ordered so? Quietly on the forest's edge a crafts-man weaves a hurdle to contain the sheep from the Downs and in another part of the green countryside a man barks newly-harvested larch poles. In a corner of some sleepy village a thatcher renovates a roof ravaged by sparrows, starlings, or mice perhaps, and on the stubbles of a cornfield harvest lingers as the strawbailer makes bales and a man builds them on a trailer. Here too, in a kind of fairy tale world of *Alice Through the Looking Glass* a little train, a miniature railway plies between Hythe and Dungeness. The spectacle of steam lives on, preserved for Gullivers in memory of the great works of Stephenson and Brunel, a time when Railways Acts were being passed year after year and the Englishman was full of enthusiasm and go.

Cricket on the green at Brockham is not a setting for a television commercial about ale, but something in the very oldest tradition of the game, the essence, in fact, of a particular religion. No matter what the claims of Yorkshiremen and Lancastrians about their Championship record, the grass roots of cricket were nurtured not far away from this little place. It all began at Hambledon in Hampshire, and went from there to Marylebone and Thomas Lord's Cricket Ground. Surrey, Kent and Sussex were there too. The rules and rituals of cricket evolved from what happened, long ago, on village greens when mutton-chopped gentlemen smoked their pipes and passed judgement on batsmen, bowlers and umpires.

The entertainment of the Morris had similar, and perhaps even more ancient origins, and for centuries has delighted English villagers in different parts of the country. A time was when it was prohibited. The Puritans looked for satanic influence everywhere and the dance was of the devil. Indeed it might, to the impressionable mind, seem to have a certain ritualistic horror even though the dancers might smile, and so the Puritans would have nothing of the kind. Dancers danced, however, the mandolin and the fiddle were

Cricket on the green at Brockham, Surrey

Cotswold Morris Dances: the Travelling Morris

played. The bells jingled in secret places. The steps, and the pattern of the dance, were not forgotten and the ritual survived to be carried round the countryside once again, and on and on, into the twentieth century, in a new revival of a mystical performance some say came from the land of the Blackamoor via Spain.

The thatcher's craft survives, despite the fact that the best materials are as hard to come by as men who know how to lay thatch on a roof. Long ago, in the wheat-growing district where straw thatches were the rule, corn was cut close to the ground with the sickle. Today, the harder end, the more durable part of the stem, is left on the stubble. The short straw of the combine, battered and crumpled, would never do for thatch. Reeds are not so easily come by because of extensive land drainage schemes and the 'improvement' in rivers and streams. The thatcher works with the best material he can lay hands on, but, like good withies for basket-making and the best

Harvesting near Mintern Magna, Wiltshire

coppice wood, such stuff as he would choose is hard to find. The thatch, when it is tidily finished, and wired against birds and mice, is a healthy covering for a roof. It breathes. It still insulates the room below from the extremes of cold, and, above all, it pleases the eye of everyone who comes upon it.

The saddest thing about the modern cornfield is the absence of colour, the 'ungregariousness' of the operations of cutting and bringing home the harvest. Once a score of men and women toiled in the field, and struggled against the threat of rain and the ruination of a crop, where now the machine crawls relentlessly from one headland to the other and back again, sometimes even after twilight, drawing moths to the headlights of the combine. The chaff is blown off. Accompanying the juggernaut is a wagon to collect the grain. The field is left with long coils of straw to be bailed and carted. In a day or two everything is done and all the countryman's yesterdays made

Thatching at Compton Chamberlayne, Wiltshire

A locomotive of the Romney, Hythe and Dymchurch Railway at Dymchurch station, Kent

Hurdle-making in Hampshire

nothing of, the gleaners of the stubbles forgotten. Perhaps it is timely to look again at the railway, even in miniature, for here at least, yesterday survives. Two hundred people may travel on the Romney, Hythe and Dymchurch, the pride of those who point to vintage steam engines, for the locomotive that bustles across the marsh at 20 miles an hour is truly a main line express engine in miniature, claimed to be the only one in the world. It is tiresome to repeat that all things change. All things do, but some not so much as others and, even if forestry has been mechanised somewhat, many of the things connected with it depend on craft and the use of hand tools. In the timber processing factories trees are rolled, when they are needed for poles, and their bark 'milled' or ground away, but where the small plantation is thinned and poles extracted there is no other way but to remove the bark manually. On the manufacturing side of timber usage it is hard to think of a machine that could do what the skilled hand of a hurdle-maker can do—or a more useful product made from copse or coppice wood.

Chopping and trimming larch poles in a Surrey wood

Of Towns and Cities

However much may be made of the pastoral scene, or even the archaeological features of that broader landscape, England's history, military, religious and cultural, really lies in its ancient cities and the architecture of their more venerable institutions. Some of the story is obvious and can be read in town walls and gates, the foundations of old abbeys, churches and forts upon which others were built. Some cities grew where the Roman legions built their forts. Some grew around the religious settlements of monks who laboured to build abbeys and great churches. The military presence encouraged the holy orders and in the course of time came the cultural centres, the great universities. Architects and masons of great skill, sometimes with the patronage of a bishop of one of the orders, and sometimes with the blessing of a king, built monuments to religious conviction, the glory of God, and to the pursuit of learning. What the Romans left encouraged the Saxons. The Normans often built where Romans and Saxons had had their strongholds, their temples and their churches. The Puritans exerted their influence in the opposite direction and probably destroyed more wonderful things than any invading nation, Danes or Vikings. We are left with works of art, with architecture on a grand scale, with sacred ruins, ancient keeps, and the tombs of soldiers and bishops, in our abbeys, and in our cathedrals. We are left with hollowed steps to dank dungeons, blackened lintel stones where fires once burned, walls breached by siege cannon and restored by the keepers of ancient monuments, battlements from which brave men fell to their death while scaling ladders were laid against them and the battering ram was used on the gate.

London, without doubt, contains the greater part of history so far as the Englishman is concerned, for it all happened here. The Romans came and went. Invaders came into the Thames by sea. The government, the king and his court, lived here. Despite the high-rise and tower block there is more here to the square mile than in any other city in England, and once this world was small, a cannon shot from Westminster and St James's, everything within the sound of Bow Bells. Fire and the plague between them almost destroyed both the city and its population when the dead were carted away day after day. At St James's Park men fought duels and gambled on the outcome of a battle royal in the cockpit. Civilization was a slow distillation, and patronage was often a part of it. Boswell dallied with his wenches in the streets. Samuel Pepys privately confessed his sins in his remarkable diary. The Tower of London is old, and Tower

Bath: the Abbey

Bridge might be thought to be older than it is, but it was built in the nineteenth century and hasn't yet had its hundredth birthday. St James's Palace, however, and the Park, are much older. Henry VIII was responsible for the building of the Palace in the early decades of the sixteenth century, and whatever else may have changed, ambassadors are still accredited to the Court of St James's. Charles I, brought up to London from Carisbrooke Castle, was promenaded through the Park to his execution in Whitehall in 1649.

St Paul's Cathedral is an important part of the history of the city. At one time it was an imposing Gothic edifice with a spire that rose 500 feet into the smoky air above the ramshackle wooden houses of the city. It was neglected during the Commonwealth. Christopher Wren was pressed into service to restore it, but his plans to do so were thwarted. Fire completed what the Puritans had willed, and Wren, his former scheme now obsolete, produced a plan from which St Paul's was rebuilt. The building occupied 38 years. The cathedral was damaged in the bombing of London in 1940 and was given a new high altar which was consecrated in 1958. The new altar was based upon Wren's original drawings.

Winchester had a similar attraction for Romans, Saxons and Normans. The Romans established themselves there. King Alfred had it as his capital. The Normans made it a place second in importance to London. Its religious significance was considerable when pilgrims came to visit the shrine of St Swithin and walked on to Canterbury. The cathedral is notable for the longest nave of any in England.

The spire of Salisbury is one of the great landmarks in that part of the world. It rises to a height of 404 feet, and the story of this great cathedral is really the story of two. When the bishoprics of Sherborne and Ramsbury were united at Old Sarum differences arose between the church and the military. The somewhat harassed secular authority

St James's Park, London

London: Tower Bridge from St Katharine's Dock Yacht Marina

upped sticks and moved to New Sarum or Salisbury. The cathedral was built in the thirteenth century and was the last of the pre-Reformation cathedrals in this country. Chilmark stone, which is warm in colour and quite beautiful in itself, was used to build Salisbury. The remarkably short time spanned by the building accounts for a positive integrity of style, the magnificence of its cloisters, nave and chapter house. Elsewhere, in the building of great churches over a century or more, architects and overseers died, funds sometimes ran out, new schemes were devised and plans altered. The result was that layered styles were particularly obvious. The work was a conglomerate of styles and periods.

York is another great city fascinating to the visitor for its architecture, its gates and walls, the Minster and the Shambles, which delight the tourist from abroad. Here, it seems, is England as it was in the days of the wool trade, and before that, when St Paulus ruled from York after the Augustinian mission to Britain. The Minster stops the visitor in his tracks but, despite its Gothic stamp, York was continually subjected to alteration and renovation, right on into the nineteenth century when the choir stalls were replaced. It is sad that

London: St Paul's Cathedral

Winchester: Kingsgate from the Close

York's decline began with the Dissolution. Its true medieval appearance changed as the old timbered buildings were pulled down to give place to Georgian houses. Paradoxically, when the wool trade ceased to be the mainstay of England's economy this great city of the north became more noted for its antiquity than its industrial importance.

Oxford and Cambridge as centres of learning have always attracted the scholars of the world. Oxford is the older university of the two, owing its origin, it is said, to an edict of Henry II who ordered English students in Paris to return to their native land. Establishing a seat of learning in England would, it was said, guarantee a succession of men of education and cultural discernment to help in the government of the country. How wise Henry II was in his generation! Magdalen Tower is Oxford's best-known landmark, but every building in the great complex of colleges is almost equally remarkable— All Souls with its beautiful towers, Merton, New College, Trinity, with places such as the Sheldonian, the Radcliffe Camera and the Ashmolean to complement them, although all three are of more recent date. Nor is Oxford without a cathedral of Norman origin, made over, first of all, by Cardinal Wolseley, and restored some 350 years later by Sir Gilbert Scott. Christopher Wren, who was professor of astronomy at Oxford at the time was engaged to design the Sheldonian as well as the library of Trinity College, Cambridge. The work of Grinling Gibbons too, graces both universities and St John's College chapel at Cambridge was designed by Sir Gilbert Scott. Hardly anywhere else, except in state and church buildings, could men of such talent have found greater scope for their gifts than in improving and embellishing the colleges associated with the two universities. Everything that was done was carried out with posterity in mind, it seems, and to stand firm forever, like the cathedrals, whether they were buildings like Trinity with its Great Court, or minor gems of architecture such as the Master's Lodge of Christ's, Cambridge.

Rochester in Kent was one of those places the Romans recognized as of strategic importance, an important place on the road—Watling Street which bridged the Medway there. Augustinians gave Rochester a certain religious significance in 604 when they established a church. The Danes came and sacked the church, and then a cathedral was built on the site. The military importance of Rochester is signified by the castle keep which dominates the town and the river as a monument, it might be said, to the failure of Simon de Montfort to take the place by force of arms.

Neither Stamford in Lincolnshire, an extraordinarily fascinating town, rich in medieval and later architecture, nor Tewkesbury in Gloucestershire lays claim to having a cathedral, qualifying either of them to be called a city. Both are steeped in history. While Stamford has a relic of a university which rebellious students from Oxford attempted to set up—Brasenose Gateway—Tewkesbury did have an abbey great church now known as the church of St Mary the Virgin. The Lancastrians were beaten at the battle of Tewkesbury in 1471. But they had their barbaric way, destroying some of the older architectural features of Stamford.

Salisbury: the Cathedral spire

Cambridge: the Master's Lodge of Christ's College

York: the medieval Shambles

Oxford: All Souls College

Stamford: St Mary's church

96

Tewkesbury, Gloucestershire; the Abbey gateway

Rochester, Kent: the Cathedral

Cambridge: the Great Court of Trinity College

Houses, Great and Small

Only a select few know what it is like to live in a mansion, set by its architect in the rural landscape, in splendid isolation from the dwellings of lesser mortals, surrounded by trees, lawns, sunken gardens, fountains, and with perhaps, the kind of natural atmosphere contrived by the genius of Capability Brown, who often put the finishing touches to a stately home. When such a home or its gardens are opened to the public visitors walk round trying to imagine what it was like long ago when none but the staff, the family and their guests walked here, and tea might be carried across the lawn to the summer house by a succession of servants. What is it like, even today on a peaceful summer's evening, beneath the cedar when there are no trippers to intrude and all that is heard is the shriek of the peacock, the cooing of the fantails or the startling clap of the woodpigeon's wings as he sails out of the plane tree? It is this kind of thing that makes the English country house and its gardens opened to the public such a draw, even if the staff may have been reduced to single figures and a liveried chaffeur, if he did appear, would look like a bit player in a black-and-white film of the 1930's. Gracious living is something obviously set off by art, sculpture, gargoyles of grotesque ugliness, mullioned windows, doors that groan on massive iron hinges, a servants' hall, a great hall with a chandelier that might rival the stars of the milky way. It is sad, most of us would admit, that life cannot go on the way it was, and when the lid is taken off what was there ceases to exist. We cannot resist looking in, although we are sometimes half ashamed at doing so, and are glad to hear that the owners are abroad. A few people, however, receive such information with regret. It would have been nice to see the kind of people who could sit calmly toying with the sole quite unconcerned with the splendour of things about them, the coats of arms, the ancient tapestry and the oil paintings of their ancestors. Such places, we are told, are really the national heritage and when they are the property of the National Trust we have a certain right to see the insides of them, but there are of course, many privately-owned houses to which the public are admitted in due season. This is usually from spring to autumn, when gardens are at their best and the visitor is footloose and fancy free to see how a wellingtonia looks in its proper setting, or discover what a ha-ha is.

The tourist has hundreds of places to choose from. The great houses advertise themselves and their attractions. Their owners sometimes stay at home and help explain to the visitor what it is all about. The National Trust publicises its work. The Tourist Board does all it can

Compton Wynyates, Warwickshire

to promote the attractions of its region, while many privately-owned houses charitably admit the gardeners to see the azaleas in early summer, the rock garden, the water garden, the fine lawn laid like baize below the terrace. There are of course the not so famous, lesser houses, and even cottages through which the tourist files, taking care not to bump his head—places like Wordsworth's cottage and his window on the world of Grasmere, or Anne Hathaway's cottage at Stratford-upon-Avon. When the tourist comes home to become an ordinary citizen once more he talks about where he has been, and what he has seen, the way the sailor talks when he is home from the sea. Have you been to Compton Wynyates, he asks, to Charlecote or to Wilton? Did you ever see anything so like a painting as Willy Lott's cottage in Suffolk, so striking as Woodhouse Eaves in Leicester where the latticed dormers look out on the gardens and the chimney stacks are works of art in themselves? Were you ever at Dedham in Essex to see the Tudor timbering of the old Master Weaver's house. There's history for you!

Capability Brown went to Charlecote to see what he could do with a landscape that was already rather grand. A lead shepherdess keeps watch over the garden and the lawn. The great house is the property of the National Trust. While Charlecote is listed as a Victorian garden, Compton Wynyates goes back to Tudor times. Some of its

Wilton House, Wiltshire

materials, brick and stone, came from the ruins of Fulbroke Castle near Warwick, and Henry VIII stayed here in his day. What adds to the striking appearance of Compton Wynyates, in addition to the fact that it stands in a hollow from which it can be viewed from the higher ground surrounding it, is the quite extraordinary layout of box and yews that stand in front of the great house. These are very fine examples of the art of topiary. Although both types of tree may be a long time growing, the Compton Wynyates trees were planted in 1885. Their layout has the regularity of chessmen on a board— a complete contrast to the kind of thing old Capability would have had if he been recruited to make changes in the grounds of this very old house. Compton Wynyates, unlike Charlecote, is privately own-ed. So too, is Wilton, in Wiltshire, but what was done here would have pleased Brown for the setting is both natural and striking. Magnificent cedars of Lebanon flank the drive. There are fine plane, lime and oak trees on the parkland. The formal garden is an impressive layout of shrubs surrounding a fountain. Sir William Chambers, who designed many of the buildings at Kew, was responsible for a stone pavilion that is part of the landscaping of Wilton put in hand by the Earl of Pembroke in the eighteenth century.

Charlecote Park, Warwickshire

Dedham, Essex: the Master Weaver's House

Woodhouse Eaves, Leicestershire: flint-and-slate cottages

Willy Lott's cottage at Flatford, on the Stour, Suffolk

Anne Hathaway's cottage, Stratford-on-Avon, Warwickshire

The Country Church

William Cobbett of the *Rural Rides* deplored the dereliction and
neglect of many country churches he encountered on his travels. He
attributed the neglect and the decline of the congregation to the
deplorable habit of some of the clergy who went off to hob-nob with
their betters at fashionable resorts. He may have been right. A
comfortable living involved being on the right side of the landowner
and the squire. The parson often rode to hounds and took an interest
in cock-fighting and even had a gamecock himself. It is more likely,
however, that Cobbett missed the point. Even in his day the towns
were drawing people from the country. Farming was hard and there
was little profit to be made in selling corn. Agricultural wages and
conditions were miserably poor. The church might have been there
since Norman times, but changes were on the way and when the
Industrial Revolution came along the depopulation of rural areas
made certain that the parson would preach to an almost empty
church. Grey's Elegy is even more significant today than when the
poet wrote it, and perhaps in this neglected spot is laid the very
fabric of the church that once was, and the essence of a world we
now conjure from the weathered inscriptions on moss-grown,
leaning headstones.

Much of the charm of the village or the hamlet derives from the
presence of the church. Like the mill, it was generally within walking
distance for those who made up the congregation, although the
landowner and his lady came in their carriage and other gentlemen
came on horseback. It is this kind of dream that makes the church so
fascinating as a relic of history, even when the congregation has
drifted away and the vicarage is no longer in use. The place has an
individuality that comes of its architectural style, the height of the
nave, the work on the choir, the timbering of the building as a
whole, the flags with which it is floored, the stone from which it was
built. Most of the old churches were, and are, cold and draughty
places, more ornamented, carpeted and tapestried, east of the chancel
rail than before it. Nor was the lighting ever very good before the
coming of electricity and on a winter's night darkness was visible at
the far end of the pew and the west end of the nave. People seem to
collect country churches and visit them to make brass rubbings, read
memorial plaques, admire the altar and the stained glass even if the
interior of the church at home is unknown to them. Out in the
country the old stone churches survived because they were out of the
way, remote in a part of the country less thoroughly scoured at a
time of persecution. The Dissolution of the monasteries was a blow

Sompting, Sussex: the Saxon church tower

against the power of Rome. The Commonwealth looked for more positive signs of idolatory than the modes and adornments of most parish churches, although a Puritan would have frowned upon the use of a hassock when a man knelt to pray. When the parish church escaped attention the Church could be thankful but there was nothing, it turned out, that it could do about the decline in the congregation except instruct an over-seeing clergyman to minister to two or three churches and serve Holy Communion first in one place and then in another. Evensong was being said to empty pews and sermons preached largely to the very young and the aged.

What makes the country church so attractive to people who go in search of them is their variety in style, shape and colour of their stonework. They have a monumental quality that derives from their isolation and even the decline in population. The churchyard is more peaceful, the nave more holy, for the silence that broods within. An owl snores in the bellfry and swifts skim past or flatten against the wall at the eaves to feed their young. The iron gate creaks and a hunting cat slips through grass the sexton's sickle didn't cut. Such things are the essence of the church in the wilderness, although some are living churches, decorated by the ladies of the parish, trafficked by the boots of young and old and the generation between, cluttered by the baskets of fruit, flowers and vegetable marrows at harvest festival and festooned with holly at Christmas time. Who wouldn't be impressed by the kind of building the Saxons and Normans put up to the glory of God at Sompting in Sussex, at Barsham in Suffolk or at Ashton-under-Hill in Worcestershire, the green path through the flowers that leads to East Qauntoxhead Church in Somerset or the relic of a monument to the glory of God at Pinkworth in Leicestershire? The wealth of church architecture lies hidden in the countryside, most of it undiscovered, most of it completely unknown to the majority of people who hurry across the rural landscape by car, like the lady in gloves, missing so much and so much.

Ashton-under-Hill, Worcestershire: fifteenth-century tower

A surviving arch of Pinkworth Abbey, Leicestershire

East Quantoxhead, Somerset: the Perpendicular church

Barsham, Suffolk: thatched nave and Norman tower

The English Country Garden

Gardens have inspired builders of great houses to extend and elaborate upon their orginal plans since the day of the Tudors. Henry VIII might have been fond of the chase and the company of ladies, but he also loved Hampton Court, yew and boxwood, the layout of shrubberies and those creations Tudor gardeners left as their monuments. Today thousands of people travel in search of the English garden between spring and autumn, although it must be said that the 'English country garden' tends to be a dream world conjured up by a song-writer. Most of the 'collectors' of gardens look for different things. Not every pilgrim goes to study plants. Some indeed, are more concerned with the architecture and the layout of the garden or its theme. Many visitors to gardens opened to the public have a specialist approach and look for pointers in the work of experts who have planned a water garden, designed an arboretum, landscaped a woodland or created a garden among established trees. There are people who love the formal garden and others who look for informality. The glory of the garden, as the poet said, is for the man who has worked in it even more than for the man who stands at the gate admiring it. The gardener knows what he has suffered cultivating and planting, rooting, grafting, persuading one thing to live in company with another, and all the setbacks and disappointments encountered along the way. Whether he has a small patch or an extensive garden of his own, he admires the achievement of others and this is almost certainly the reason why so many people take advantage of the opportunity to visit gardens opened to the public.

In a day when domestic staff could be engaged for little more than their keep the owners of great houses had no shortage of hands to do the work in the garden. There were gardeners and under-gardeners, apprentices and garden boys to tend the plants, to cultivate the lawns, trim the boxwood hedge, weed between the flags, plant and transplant, pot and pot-up. Designers were given their head to plan complex patterns. The plants themselves were put in in ranks and rows of carefully selected herbs and perennials. The approach to a fountain might be set with symmetrical cobbles or flagged massively with local stone. Pools would be created and vast and pretentious schemes of topiary put in hand—until they outgrew and outlived the men who conceived them, rising higher and keeping the gardeners busy. Relics of the great days of formality in garden design tell of a different outlook so far as expenditure was concerned, but the cost of upkeep surely resulted in a change in the end and a preference for

In the walled garden at Mottisfont Abbey, Hampshire

natural landscaping, terraced lawns, and fewer urns or ewers of heavy stone on paths along which the master of the house and his lady might leisurely promenade. Everyone who goes in search of a particular style or kind of garden can find it somewhere in the English counties, and if not in the great botanical or municipal gardens, in one opened in due season to the visitor.

Two well-known gardens in Kent attract their share of visitors— Walmer and Sissinghurst. Both date from Tudor times. Walmer Castle is one of the forts put up by Henry VIII when he feared invasion from the Continent but the garden is of a much later date and was, in fact, laid out by Lady Hester Stanhope in 1805. Sissinghurst, which qualifies as a castle by virtue of its tower, was really a Tudor mansion which fell derelict. It was restored when it was acquired by the late Sir Harold Nicolson and his wife Vita Sackville-West who set about the formidable task of laying it out in a formal style. The White Garden at Sissinghurst is remarkable in its effect, being planted with silver-leaved and white flowering plants. The rose garden is stocked with old-fashioned, scented roses which many rose-lovers cherish with nostalgia when flamboyant colour and a new shape have banished the scented cabbage rose. Sissinghurst is renowned as a garden for all seasons, the Nicolsons having planned it with this in mind.

Mottisfont Abbey in Hampshire is really a Georgian house built on the site of an Augustinian priory, one of those that fell in ruin after the Dissolution of the monasteries. It is owned by the National Trust who were responsible for the creation of a fine rose garden in what was once a walled kitchen garden. Mottisfont has fine cedars, planes, beeches and an avenue of pleached limes. To the north, at Stratford-upon-Avon is another sort of garden at Hall's Croft where Shakespeare's daughter lived, one of the places administered by the Shakespeare Birthplace Trust.

There are of course, a great many gardens of less renown in terms of history, all of them places of great charm. The camera tells its story of such gardens—at the Greyhound at Tidmarsh in Berkshire, the courtyard of the Shaven Crown at Shipton-under-Wychwood in Oxfordshire, Cobblers at Crowborough in Sussex, Tumber House at Headley, Gilridge at Kingswood, both in Surrey.

Hall's Croft, Stratford-upon-Avon, Warwickshire

Beneath the walls of Walmer Castle, Kent

Sissinghurst, Kent: the Rose Garden

Roses at the Greyhound Inn, Tidmarsh, Kent

Wallflowers in the courtyard of the Shaven Crown Inn, Shipton-under-Wychwood, Oxfordshire

Lupins and marguerites at Cobblers, Crowborough, Sussex

A wall of rock plants at Tumber House, Headley, Surrey

The peony border, at Gilridge, Kingswood, Surrey